Palindrome

Krithiga Arul

BookLeaf
Publishing

India | USA | UK

Presentation by *BookLeaf Publishing*

Web: www.bookleafpub.com

E-mail: info@bookleafpub.com

ISBN: 9789358318227

First edition 2024

DEDICATION

Ranjani Arul, My sister, without your constant
push, this book is just a dream.

And to writers' block, which made me feel I
would never get to write a single word again.
Sorry! I won again. Better luck next time.

PREFACE

After years of trying to pen words on paper, accounting for my writer's block, I challenged myself with something unique. Here is my try at palindrome poetry, Mirroring nature within them, which can be read from top to bottom and also from bottom to top.

I have also done something witty with each poem. If you've figured it out, don't forget to reach out to me about it.

Moon

Moon; my loving Luna, for you'll be there ;even if I can't see
When I feel the light, amidst the dark sea
My grunting pain turns into a glittering glee
Through thy musing, that amuses me

When I see you, I know I'll be fine
After shedding cries of rain
Beholding secrets sorrows of mine
Stories behind my silent pain

Even when you're broken; 'you be beautiful'
Always half seen, yet so powerful
Stains of yours, something much more meaningful
Do you know your valor? It's highly doubtful!

Close to me, yet so far
Could you make me as peaceful as you are?
Stillness of yours, can soothe my scar
When I stroll alone, gazing stars.

(*Read it again backwards*)

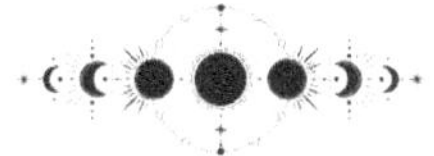

Star

Star, can I be you for the night?
When at will; I can be out of sight
Fighting fears, fueling fright
Escaping reality by taking flight

Souls that wanders; finds in you, a pole star
For lost hope, you light up like dog star
Missing and missed luck, you're a wishing star
To love and laughter, you're a shining star

Born out of a breakdown, nobody will oversee
You're a twinkling delight, every one will agree
You light up even the apogee
You're a sight to behold, fireflies on the sea.

(*Read it again backwards*)

Sea

Sea, wondering how you wash worries, while you wave
Hiding silent storms as you rave
Pearls are your gift; for those who are brave
Salts are your secrets, that you sincerely save

The smell of yours is something that I deify
Voice of yours, touches my soul high
Vast are the horizons, hiding something that you mystify
Do you really reflect only the sky?

(*Read it again backwards*)

Sky

Sky, you're more like a painter's brush;
Colors that you create when lights crush
Turning strokes with a sudden gush
Painting duple, like a song thrush

Purpul is the stroke, for calm after the storm
Abendrot over the horizon, as dawn; withholding the qualm
Azure of eternity is an everlasting calm
Grey on hazy day awaiting a rainy bomb

'Akaya' is the limit, nobody will ever doubt
Serenely sole for all of us, the crowds
Omnipotent you're, scaring douds
Painting yourself with arteries of clouds

(*Read it again backwards*)

Cloud

Clouds, oh! Wisdom you teach: lemme relish
You amuse at least one soul; minutes before you perish
Importance of yours, that nobody could blemish
Lover of lone sky whom he cherishes

Turning transparent is what you teach
Forms of yours, carrying, message each
Adapting to your surrounding, is what you preach
Hold your strength tight and shower only when and where
                                        it should reach

For the secret that you hold; tell me does it pain
Without you, earth is nothing but a vain
For the crepuscular ray, you act as a vein
A melody on the meadows, while you rain.

(*Read it again backwards*)

Rain

Rain, will you wash away my pain?
Even, when there's nothing you'll gain
Seeking happiness; nothing but in vain
A rainbow awaits - I have been Lain.

With thunderous beats, you muffle my cry
Even when I'm wringing wet, my heart is dry
An alien in the pour; even if I pry
A silent smiling storm, with a wry

Racing through the window, as you flow
Promising sunshine for tomorrow
Cleansing souls, by the ballad that you blow
I start, strolling after storm; searching for rainbow.

(*Read it again backwards*)

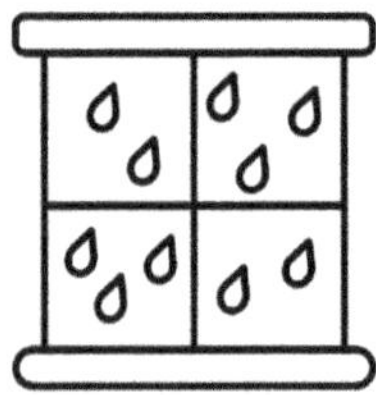

Rainbow

Rainbow, where have you been?
Hiding the magic that you spin
Ensuring enlightenment, within
An In and out, boundless being

Taking upon voyage, for your golden pot
Bridge between, as of now, not having a stopping spot
Promise of the sky; one must not swat
With your hues; the smiles that we got

Shades of yours are in itself a mirth
Arc of awakening is an amusing rebirth
Shining shades, against the sparkling dew; is a dearth
Probing pristine, in whole of the earth.

(*Read it again backwards*)

Earth

Earth, oh! You're the mother of miracles
All that you offer, is no less than empirical
Welcoming wonders with lullaby, so lyrical
With millions to offer and much more, you must be mystical

While finding myself, I'm lost in your view
Mount Everest, Dead sea, Northern lights to name a few
White sand; Stone forest, Marble cave and mountain dew
Exploring you, I'll always ends up in discovering something new

Home you're for someone like me
Shrine at every step, is all I can see
The only living force; how wonderful can you be?
Thinking under the shadow of a tree.

(*Read it again backwards*)

Tree

Tree, teach me the techniques of determination
You're one among of, nature's divine creation
Resisting a whirlwind; standing tall on your foundation
'Fall, but raise again' you live by this demonstration

Magical, truly you're; for you'll live, even in a tiny space you find
You get so little of what you give in return; may I also be, that kind
Rustling of your leaves, on a breezy night calms my mind
May I stand still, like you; however hard, might be the wind.

(*Read it again backwards*)

Wind

Wind, will you let me see
Adventures of yours; through the tree
Sharing secrets; while I pass by thee
Gushing through at will, traveling free

Concealed but concerned, having no qualm
Brushing the bushes, like a burst of bomb
Painting over the plains, rustling calm
Standing silently starting a storm.

(*Read it again backwards*)

Strom

Storm, throw me with more tribulation
For, nobody can fight my foundation
With your soaring wind, shove me in any situation
Every disaster you drive; I'm one step away, from my destination

There's nothing stopping me, from being an achiever
Fierce like you; 'My best, I will deliver'
Flood or quake, there's nothing I quiver
On every obstacle, I will flow like a river.

(*Read it again backwards*)

River

River, guide me the way; you glide through the barrier
Withholding elegance and all the more classier
As healing tirthas, making life more happier
Calling changes , peace and as life carrier

A mind like a river, I would recall
Transient; yet a calmness that befall
Forever flourishing, having no forestall
Flowing from a cascade to form a waterfall.

(*Read it again backwards*)

Waterfall

Waterfall, I envy the way you flow
Taking calculating steps, too slow
To hit the ground with a hammering blow
How far have you traveled only you know

Share the silent struggle that you faced
While warring fears which you chased
Marathoning miles, that you raced
Leaving the pains that you braced

For my ink to flow; aiming at August
Warring my inner monster for the longest
Unstoppable and overwhelming; daringly darkest
The mind is nothing, but a maze in a forest.

(*Read it again backwards*)

Forest

Forest, while I stroll along the solitude of the trees
Calming my soul, with your blowing breeze
Wandering windy woods, is where I find my peace
Cradling my chaotic mind, that comes to cease

Behind the bemusing melody, is where I bloom
Walking on withering leaves while I groom
Lore of yours; that I wish to carry, beyond my tomb
Whilst you bear me like in a mother's womb

Healing my heart; that was once hollow
By your enchanted wind, which follows
Reborn I'm, leaving behind my darkest shadow
As I walk, heading towards the meadows.

(*Read it again backwards*)

Meadows

Meadows, oh! Carpet of wild flowers
Buzzing with bees, during the golden hour
Scorching sunlight, that slowly showers
Soaring silently, until late summer holding power

Walking through the velvety hyland
Nourished with a natural lullaby; so grand
Hearing hooting owls, night at hand
Standing in the middle of a yellow island.

(*Read it again backwards*)

Island

Island, precious jewel; scattered through ocean wave
A calming refuge for which I crave
Facing my fears, will I be brave?
Freezing my racing thoughts, as I rave

Lost paradise you're; creating calm that's for certain
Confusing thoughts of mine, clouded like a curtain
Solitude of yours, spreading happiness like a spring fountain
Raising from the sea of mind, like a mountain.

(*Read it again backwards*)

Mountain

Mountain, oh! heavens on high
Adobe of god, in the midst of sky
Withholding virtues of life, unshakenly high
Bending the ways between earth and sky

Diving deep lies in you; a divine dwelling
You preach me the power of persistent trying
Conquering war, with consistent climbing
Introducing me to the warrior within, who has been hiding

Taking steps of hope, so slow
Hearing whispers, that flows
Over the hill, sparkling stars that glow
Lost in mountains, capped with snow.

(*Read it again backwards*)

Snow

Snow, how pure you are
Sparkles of snow are earth adorned by star
Screening my sage old scar
Flakes of uniqueness falling from afar

Frosting the earth, for us to admire
Falling as first snow, marking a creative state to transpire
Burning my cold soul, that I dire
Calling in calmness, over my cold fire.

(*Read it again backwards*)

Fire

Fire; you're a spark, that's been neglected
Like a mind, that's been mostly unattended
Like wild fire, that has been tempted
Chaos in calm, that has gotten ignited

Powerful source of energy that flows
Profound passion and courage that you show
Maintaining balance, yet nobody's foe
Lush lands are love; formed by the fire of Volcano.

(*Read it again backwards*)

Volcano

Volcano, how come we be alluringly alike
Storing suppressed screams, ready to strike
Magmas of mind, that are about to hike
Lava meltdowns, which I dotingly dislike

Melting away ring of fire; a races of mind, that I have won
Renewing energy like I have never done
Sizzling sonnet that I spun
Illuminating the sky with fire reaching the sun.

(*Read it again backwards*)

Sun

Sun, I have heard hanuman was there
To reach you, while nobody would ever dare
Why are you always glazing glare?
To face you, even the fierce will fear

Some source of wisdom, will you spare
Enlightenment as illumination, which you share
Heat of life is what you wear
Symbolizing stern grandeur of justice; you swear

You burn away all my negativity
Like fusing nuclear power with your high density
A ray of hope, a promising possibility
Sunshine of yours, pouring positivity

Souring summer solstice, in the month of June
You make the song bird croon
Only source of light, for the flowers to bloom
Sun on the horizon; meeting the moon.

(*Read it again backwards*)